W9-BVC-603

HIGH-TECH JOBS

VIDEO GAME DESIGN

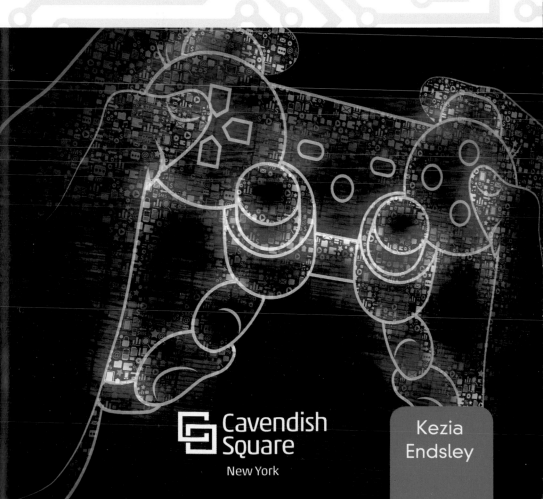

Cavendish
Square
New York

Kezia
Endsley

To Piper, Christopher, & Ryan. All my love.

Published in 2015 by Cavendish Square Publishing, LLC
243 5th Avenue, Suite 136, New York, NY 10016

Library of Congress Cataloging-in-Publication Data

Endsley, Kezia.
Video game design / Kezia Endsley.
pages cm. — (High-tech jobs)
Includes bibliographical references and index.
ISBN 978-1-50260-113-1 (hardcover) ISBN 978-1-50260-118-6 (ebook)
1. Computer games—Programming—Vocational guidance. 2. Computer games—Design—Vocational guidance.
I. Title.

QA76.76.C672E53 2015
794.8'1536—dc23

2014024962

Editor: Kristen Susienka
Copy Editor: Cynthia Roby
Art Director: Jeffrey Talbot
Senior Designer: Amy Greenan
Senior Production Manager: Jennifer Ryder-Talbot
Production Editor: David McNamara
Photo Researcher: J8 Media

Printed in the United States of America

CONTENTS

Being a video game designer can be both challenging and fun.

INTRODUCTION TO VIDEO GAME DESIGN

What do video game designers actually do on the job? What kind of skills and educational background do you need to succeed in this field? How much can you expect to make, and what are the pros and cons of this field? Does this career path have a future? Is it even the right career for you?

This book can help you answer these questions by explaining the roles of video game designers, how you can prepare for a career in the field, how to break into the field, and how to become a successful video game designer. Video game design is a lucrative career with a real future. It's also very competitive. This book can be your first step in preparing to smash your competition.

BORN FROM DESIRE AND FORGED OF NECESSITY

Some argue that the first "real" video game created was *Tennis for Two* (1958), while others say it was Atari's *Pong* (1972). *Pong* might be accurately described as the "first successful" video game,

The Sears Tele-Games Atari Pong console, released in 1975.

but it wasn't the first gone by far. The history of video game design, as it pertains to a career interest, actually started when people began to hold paying jobs with the goal of making video games for others to play.

The consumer market for video games was born with the release of home computers such as the Apple II and as the Atari 2600 video game console. The Atari 2600 had no hard drive to store programs, virtually no **random access memory (RAM)**, and **read-only memory (ROM)** game cartridges with only two to four kilobytes of memory. The real challenge for game developers was working around the technical limitations of the systems and code and creating something that users liked and wanted to keep playing.

The early 1980s was the golden age of Atari, with its ultimate demise and breakup in 1983. Rebuilding began after the "video game crash of 1983." By the mid-1980s the video game industry began to evolve at a fast pace. In 1985, the Nintendo Entertainment System was released in North America.

Nintendo is largely responsible for reviving the video game industry, due mainly to its successful series, Super Mario Bros.

The 1990s became the golden age of computer video games in general, with marked innovation, including the move from raster to 3-D graphics. The 1990s gave rise to a large number of game developers, such as Activision, known for *Crash Bandicoot* and *Spiro the Dragon*, Electronic Arts, which made *The Sims* series, Blizzard, the makers of the *StarCraft* and *Warcraft* series, and id Software, creators of *Doom* and *Quake*. Video game design then was greatly advanced with the creation of 3-D elements.

The 2000s showed innovation on both consoles and PCs, and an increasingly competitive market for portable game systems. During this time, Sega exited the hardware market. Nintendo, with its GameCube, fell behind. Sony, with its PlayStation, solidified its lead in the industry, and Microsoft developed a gaming console (the Xbox). Nintendo would later return to the forefront with its Wii console.

The Atari 2600 video game console was a huge success in the early 1980s.

The rise of casual, social media-type games, which began on PCs, would be the next big development in game design. **Casual games** have limited complexity and are designed for shortened or impromptu play sessions. These casual games would find a huge niche in the mobile market. Companies such as Maxis, which made *The Sims*, PopCap, the maker of *Bejeweled*, and Zynga, with its game *Happy Farm*, would benefit as a result. Even more recent developments include the use of **cloud computing**.

> ## " "
> ## *You have to reinvent yourself in this business every five or ten years, because everything changes so quickly.*
>
> MARK CERNY, VIDEO GAME
> INDUSTRY PATRIARCH

THE VIDEO GAME MARKET TODAY

Game design today is not as much about how to write and test the code as it is about carrying out the vision of the creative director. The technology continues to move into the background, and is increasingly becoming invisible to the players. The future is a game that is continuously updated in the background without the players being aware or inconvenienced. The developer's job is to use technology to make that happen.

Video game design has reinvented itself many times throughout the decades. The market today, via mobile devices or consoles, is healthy and thriving. Before you pursue a career in video game design be sure that you are comfortable with change. In fact, you should welcome it. The field of video game design will morph many times over during your lifetime, and you need to be open and ready to grow and change along with it. You have to always be open to learning new ways of doing things.

A CAREER IN VIDEO GAME DESIGN

The modern video game design career is often split into several different job descriptions. For example, the game designer builds a detailed **design document** and closely oversees the game's progress throughout its life. The game writer is responsible for writing the game's story, the character dialogue, game tips, menu text, and cutting scene or narration text. The game artist creates visual materials for the game's design and development, including characters, world environments, creatures, weapons, vehicles, and objects. The game programmer does the nitty-gritty work of writing and testing the code. You would likely become part of a large team of people with the same or similar titles.

Collaboration and communication skills are important if you want to work in this field. Designers rarely work alone.

WHERE SHOULD YOU START?

Are you more interested in the art and visual aspects of a game, or feel that you would be great at creating the narrative? Do you enjoy programming code, or would you rather design a game that someone else codes?

You don't need to know the answers to these questions yet. In order to find the best fit for yourself in the game design industry, you need to understand how the job and industry work.

Gamers at the 2013 Game Developers Conference in San Francisco, California.

Video Game Design

1 A CAREER IN VIDEO GAME DESIGN: THE BIG PICTURE

B ecoming a professional video game designer is within your grasp, and it can be a lucrative and enjoyable career. In terms of pay and satisfaction, it was rated fifteenth of the top 100 jobs by *CNNMoney*. There's no doubt that it's a desirable profession, yet it's also highly competitive. Since you're reading this book, you must be somewhat serious about learning how to succeed in this field. Your goal at this point should be to get as much experience in making and designing games as you can. In the process, decide which of two main paths you want to take: the artistic or the mathematical approach to gaming. Both are important and necessary. Choosing a path that complements your interests and natural abilities will lead to greater success. However, make an effort to understand the other at a less specific level. Keep in mind that even if you follow the artistic path, a solid programming background is a must for success in this field.

Game programming isn't just about coding or creating awesome graphics. It's about delivering something to your players that they want to come back and play again. The best game developers know their audience. They also understand how to translate their audience's needs and desires into a great player experience. When you're creating games, it's critical to keep the players in mind. If that's a fun and exciting challenge, you're in the right place. Read on!

Of course some degree of artistic talent and creativity is necessary to craft a great game. Here's something you should know. It's a common misconception that you're either born with creativity or not. Some people naturally are more creative than others. However, these are also skills that you can sharpen on the job. Just like any muscle, your "creative" muscle will get stronger the more you use it.

What about those math and programming skills? The truth is that all video game designers, even the game artists, must have a strong set of programming and video graphics skills. To work in the world of video game design, you must be knowledgeable about computer programming and comfortable and adept at writing software, which involves an understanding of algebra and geometry.

Before you become too overwhelmed about all the details video game designers are supposed to know and tasks they are to perform, take a closer look at how video game design came about and how it works today. After that, you'll learn a bit about what video game designers do on the job, and how to best prepare for success.

THE ORIGINS OF THE VIDEO GAME MARKET

As you read earlier, when video games were first created, the developer's biggest challenge involved getting around the hardware and software limitations of that time. In the very beginning, in the pure hardware environment, developers just had to build the game and determine whether they liked it. If they were dissatisfied with the gameplay, they had to build another

Pac-Man is considered a classic of the arcade game medium and an icon of 1980s pop culture.

motherboard with different chips and give it another go. Coming from that environment, developers were thrilled when the technology improved, and they just needed to make a code change and then wait "only" fifteen minutes or more to see its effects!

The world of video game design began with the merging of four significant trends: the popularity of traditional role-playing (RPG) and strategy games, the success of arcade video games, the boom in affordable home computing, and the huge success of home consoles such as the Atari 2600.

A role-playing game is a type of video game in which the player controls the actions of one or more main characters, who live and resolve some kind of conflict in a fictional world. A strategy game is a type of game that requires clever thinking and planning to advance and achieve victory. These games contain strategic, tactical, and sometimes logistical challenges.

Atari's Significance in the Early Days of Video Games

Nolan Bushnell and Ted Dabney founded Atari in 1972. Their first product was the arcade game *Pong*. In 1974, Atari made its move into the home console market with a home version of *Pong*. From 1972 to 1983, Atari was the nexus of creativity and genius for all things video games. Many great minds found their way to Atari that decade.

Some quick facts about Atari:

- In 1976, Steve Wozniak and Steve Jobs worked on *Breakout* and other projects for Atari before leaving the company to form Apple Inc.

- The Atari 2600 debuted in 1977 and sold for $199. Throughout its lifetime, 25 million units were sold. This created an incredible demand for video games. Many competitors were created from its success. The Atari 2600 was inducted into the National Toy Hall of Fame in 2007.

- The Atari 5200 system, released in 1982, was in direct competition with the ColecoVision. Unfortunately, the system wasn't backward compatible, meaning compatible with previous versions of the software. This meant users could not use games for the 2600 on the 5200.

- Atari is viewed as being largely responsible for the "video game crash of 1983," whereby video game revenues dropped 97 percent from 1983 to 1985. Although there were

several reasons for the crash, the main cause was saturation of the market with hundreds of low-quality games, the most infamous being the *E.T.* video game, that were released mainly by Atari. Nintendo Entertainment Systems and its Super Mario Bros. series revived the market in 1985.

- The Atari 7800 was released in 1986 and sold at $140. This was during Nintendo Entertainment System's heyday. The 7800 enjoyed little success even though Atari had included backward compatibility with the Atari 2600.

- Atari released a few more gaming systems including a handheld system, Lynx, in 1989 and priced at $190. Although considered graphically superior to the Nintendo Game Boy, it stood no chance of success against the market dominance of the Nintendo brand.

- The last gaming system Atari released was called Atari Jaguar (1993). Selling for $250, it was marked to compete with Sony's first-generation PlayStation and the Sega Saturn.

In 2013, Atari Inc. filed for bankruptcy. The company emerged one year later and entered the social casino gaming industry with Atari Casino. Frédéric Chesnais, head of the company, stated that its entire operations consist of a staff of ten people. It was a rather sad end to the company that arguably "started it all."

Each trend took place at the end of the 1970s and early 1980s. During this time, the typical game designer likely worked on a very small team, creating games such as *Adventure*, *Combat*, *Pac-Man*, *Space Invaders*, and *Missile Command*, all for Atari. Designers might also have worked for independent developers and distributors of video games, such as Activision, which created *Pitfall!* for the Atari 2600 in 1982.

Fast-forward a few years. Atari is slowly moving out of the picture and Nintendo is emerging as an industry leader. The industry begins the move from raster to 3-D graphics and from 8-bit to 16-bit games. Video game design is greatly advanced with the creation of 3-D elements. Many companies were formed during these decades, and teams of fifty to sixty people might work on one video game for close to a year. A career in game design is no longer an esoteric hobbyist endeavor.

The 1990s gave rise to several genres of video games, including the **first-person shooter (FPS)**, real-time strategy, survival horror, and **massively multiplayer online games (MMO or MMOG)**. Handheld gaming soared in popularity throughout the decade, thanks in part to Nintendo's Game Boy. Arcade games, although still relatively popular in the early 1990s, began to decline as home consoles and home PCs became more common.

THE ROLE OF THE INDIE GAME PROGRAMMER

The indie, or "bedroom," programmer has always been an important force in the video game industry, although his or her success and opportunities have ebbed and flowed with industry trends. In the early 1990s, PCs were the domain of the tinkerer and the business professional. Thanks to the crash of 1983, PCs were also the only major outlet for North American game design. The problem was that they were built for business rather than leisure.

After a decade of hacking and add-ons, the hardware reached a level where a bedroom programmer could attempt the fast-paced action of arcade and console games. Add to that a growing

Two people playing together on a Sony PlayStation video game system.

network of dial-up boards, and you have distribution. Creativity exploded, giving rise to games such as *Commander Keen*, *Jill of the Jungle*, and *Doom*.

In the mid-1990s, the Internet hit the mainstream. All of those bulletin boards dried up, so there was no distribution. At the same time, 3-D cards began to hit. File sizes increased, coding became more complicated, and development was suddenly more expensive. As PCs became somewhat of a household appliance, the competition became about the "fanciest" showpiece. For about a decade, the bedroom developers all but vanished.

Then in the mid-2000s, thanks to the growth of social networking and the advance of boxed game design kits like Mark Overmars' *Game Maker*, a new generation of bedroom developers surfaced.

The rise of mobile gaming has been a benefit to aspiring game designers. Anyone with an idea, and time, patience, and know-how, can create a game and upload it to Apple's App Store or to Google Play, for example, and then get immediate, massive exposure. The market has come full circle. It's not just the "little guy" who is benefitting from this trend. Casual games have found a huge niche in the mobile market, and companies such as Maxis, which created *The Sims*, PopCap, which is known for *Bejeweled*, and Zynga, which started with *Happy Farm*, have benefitted as a result.

Crowd-funding sites such as **Kickstarter** have also changed the landscape for getting games published. Gaming was Kickstarter's largest funded category in 2012, raising $83 million for successfully funded projects. Because of these factors, the indie scene is once again one of the most vibrant regions of the development community. That's good news for you.

It's important to know the history of video game design. Think of it as learning to walk before you can run. With perspective on where video game design came from, you'll be better able to create the next big thing! If nothing else, you can use your knowledge to impress others. Nothing shows dedication and real interest in a career like knowing and understanding its history.

A CAREER IN MODERN-DAY VIDEO GAME DESIGN

The modern video game design career comes in several variations, depending on experience and skills. Consider each of these career paths a bit more closely and think about your skills and interests:

Game designer: An experienced game developer, the game designer creates a detailed design document outlining all aspects of the game's design, gameplay, interface, and world. They update the design document continuously throughout development. Designers follow the current build of the game very closely, often incorporating tester feedback into design decisions. The job requires intimate knowledge of games, unending creativity, solid writing, and good organization and collaboration skills.

Mechanics designer: The mechanics designer designs rules for

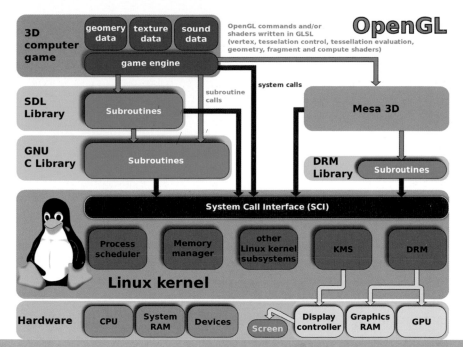

the gameplay and ensures that they remain balanced throughout the game. This person is also known as a systems designer.

Level designer: The level designer is responsible for designing levels, missions, and environments, often placing elements of terrain that are designed by the environment artists.

Writer: The writer writes the game's story, the character dialogue, the cut scene or narration text, game tips, and menu text. Writers must work closely with other designers to follow their plan for the game.

Lead designer: A lead designer must be experienced in all aspects of game design and uses this status to lead a team of game designers. The lead designer works closely with other department leads and gets the final say on all major design choices. Many high-profile lead designers are responsible for the game idea. It's common for the lead designer to reveal the game at trade shows and answer media questions.

Game artist: The game artist produces visual materials for the game's design and development, including characters, world environments, creatures, weapons, vehicles, and objects. This person also creates highly polished visual arts for promoting the game and influencing customer impressions. Game artist jobs account for up to nearly one-third of the game development team. Game artists are often, though not necessarily always, skilled in both 2-D and 3-D art. Versatility will increase your job prospects.

Game programmer: The game programmer is one of the most difficult parts of video game development and one with the most frequent job openings. Many entry-level jobs are for small tasks requiring programmers, so it can be a great way to break into the gaming industry even if programming isn't your major. There are some self-taught programmers, but normally you must have a bachelor's degree in subjects such as computer science, 3-D mathematics, or physics. Most video and computer games are based on C++ or C, but Java is very common for mobile and browser games to enable cross-platform support.

If you are interested in video game design but you don't know which of these areas is best for you, continue reading. You will learn more about each of these areas, including the skills and education necessary to excel in them.

YOUR FIRST VIDEO GAME DESIGNER JOB: GAME PROGRAMMER

Did you know that people who visualize success are more likely to achieve it? With that in mind, picture yourself in a few years. You've just graduated from college with a degree in computer science and, after some job-searching and living at home for a while, you've landed your first job at "Gaming Games, Inc.," a (fictitious) video game developer and publisher.

You majored in computer science and 3-D math and spent those extra nights making sure you understood your algebra and physics courses. The summer internship with the local game developer that you worked hard to get has proved beneficial. You got your foot in the door by being hired as a game programmer. Also, you are already familiar with creating games for Android or iOS devices. Through gaining proficiency in using C++ during your college years, you have created your own games.

It's because of your familiarity and comfort with these or comparable languages and programs, and your great personality and enthusiasm, of course, that you landed this entry-level position as "junior game programmer." Of course, you realize that hot technologies come and go, and you're committed to keeping up with the latest cool trends, languages, and tools. In fact, you enjoy doing this.

At Gaming Games, Inc., you'll be working with the creative director and lead game designer, who provide you with the design document for the new game they are developing. The design document contains prototypes for aspects of the game, such as backgrounds and characters, and the lead programmer will instruct you and your team in the coding process for making these prototypes "come to life."

During the development phase, the team of game designers begins by fleshing out initial character art, levels, and story. Next, the team begins to envision the player experience by outlining the user interface, missions, combat systems, artificial intelligence, and game modes. These are the nuts and bolts that provide the operational foundation of the game.

The design team will give you and your team direction about the portions of the game they need coded. It's your job as part of the team to create and test this high-level game code. For this task you'll be using C++.

In addition to coding in C++, you'll use Gaming Games'

The Most Commonly Used Programming Languages in Game Development

Whether you're just getting started with programming or have been coding for a while, it's important that you be aware of the most commonly used programming languages.

- **C++** is a general-purpose **object-oriented programming (OOP) language** that is freeform, meaning spaces do not matter when writing code, and compiled, which means it creates machine code from **source code**. It is the most widely used language, especially in console video games, and has numerous tools developed for it. The downside is that it's large, complicated, and has potentially long compilation times.

- **C#** (pronounced "see-sharp") is an object-oriented language created by Microsoft based in large part on C++. It has automatic **memory management** but is generally limited to Microsoft platforms, such as Windows and Xbox, and is easily **reverse-engineered**.

- **Java** is an object-oriented language that has automatic memory management, but lacks user-defined value types, is not available on major gaming consoles, and is easily reverse-engineered. It was originally designed for developing programs for handheld devices but later became a popular choice for creating web applications.

- **Objective-C** is a general-purpose, object-oriented language based on the C language and used by Apple for its OS X and iOS. If you plan on creating iPhone, iPad, and Mac apps, you need a working understanding of Objective-C.

- **Scripting languages**, such as Lua, Python, and Ruby, are often used for gameplay but not for the bulk of the game code itself.

These languages don't include other tools you might use, such as an **integrated development environment (IDE)**, to develop the source code and other in-house prototype and asset conversion tools, which are programs that change artwork, for example, into the game's custom format. Some custom tools may even be delivered with the game, such as a level editor.

Example of the programming language code C++.

own tools and **application programming interfaces (APIs)**. You already had basic experience using **debuggers** and are familiar with the concept of **version control**, so this will not be a difficult transition. You'll be coding, initially, at a high level, so it's important that you come into the position with a lot of enthusiasm. The game designers and lead designers you work with put in their hours of programming and debugging as part of learning their trade and "paying their dues," and you'll need to do the same. That experience will be invaluable in moving up the ladder at Gaming Games, Inc.

Of course, there are other ways that you could get your foot in the door at Gaming Games, Inc. Perhaps you created an amazing mobile game that went viral on the App Store, or you have amassed a collection of your own games and have a reputation for being an amazing indie programmer. The example described here is the most common and well-mapped-out way to get your foot in the door. Basically, you must major in computer science and immerse yourself in C++.

> ## " "
> *Programming is a necessity in this industry, but a background in programming can lead to a lot of opportunities in areas of project management.*
>
> ARSENY LEBEDEV, MANAGING DIRECTOR OF
> SIGNUS LABS IN NEW YORK

PREPARING FOR A CAREER IN VIDEO GAME DESIGN

It's never too soon to begin preparing for your career. In fact, knowing what you want to do is the first step. If you already know you want to be a game developer, you're way ahead of many of your peers. Having solid career goals gives you a real advantage. Begin working now on learning what you need to know. Here is a sampling of what game companies will want to see in an entry-level hire:

- **A working knowledge of C++.** Be comfortable with the C++ language. Knowing the syntax and compiling "Hello world" isn't good enough. A class in college isn't going to be enough, either. You need to use C++ in some significant projects—either your own projects or in some term projects at school. For example, you should be able to discuss the order in which destructors are called for classes with inheritance, and have the ability to define "const-correctness" and why it is a good idea.

- **Knowledge of basic 3-D linear algebra.** As an entry-level programmer, you'll most likely work extensively on high-level game code at first. To do things effectively, you'll need a good understanding of the fundamentals of 3-D linear

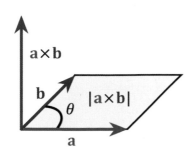

algebra. Make sure you know your dot and cross products, how to calculate them, but most importantly, what they represent and when you should use them. Become comfortable with relative coordinate systems and matrices as transforms. Calculating whether an object in the world is within a certain distance from the player, and within a certain angle of its aiming direction, should be close to second nature.

You really will use your math skills, including algebra, if you choose a career in video game design.

- **Basic knowledge of gaming tools.** You should be familiar with version control, know how to use a debugger, and so on.

- **Strong desire to continue to learn and update your skills.** In this ever-changing industry, you will constantly learn new platforms, APIs, languages, approaches, new styles, and more. It's great to be confident in your skills, but you also have to show interest in learning new things.

- **A bachelor's degree in computer science or similar subject.** You won't learn everything you need to know in college, of course, but earning a degree shows prospective employers that you can stick to something for four years and be successful. You'll be developing and fine-tuning those math and computer science skills along the way.

Each of these is discussed further in Chapter 2. If you want to get started now, download an open source game project of the language you are going to use. Look for a well-written **codebase**

> **My advice for the novice is that you should start making video games. All the information of how to do it is right there on the Internet. Anybody can download Unity or GameSalad and get started.**
>
> JESSE SCHELL, SCHELL GAMES

for a simple game, and then study how the codebase is laid out. One of the best ways to learn game development is to analyze the codebase's foundation and start tinkering with the code instead of writing out the code one by one. Then start taking it apart and adding your own code.

Analyzing an open source game project eliminates a lot of the guesswork of what you still need to know to program a game. If you know *Pong*, for example, you'll have a better understanding about writing a simple arcade shooter game. The goal is to improve and deepen your conceptual understanding with every game you write.

After that, you'll be ready to download free products such as Unity or GameSalad and get started making your own games. Unity is a cross-platform game engine with a built-in IDE developed by Unity Technologies. It is a flexible and reusable software program providing all the functionality necessary to develop a game. It is used to develop video games for web plug-ins, desktop platforms, consoles, and mobile devices.

The best way to learn when it comes to creating video games is to learn by doing.

GameSalad, which has a "free-to-make" model, is aimed primarily at non-programmers for composing games in a drag-and-drop fashion using visual editors. You can visit gamesalad.com for more information.

You can't possibly know all there is to know about video game design when you interview, and employers don't expect their entry-level employees to know that much. What you want to convey to a potential employer is that you have a real enthusiasm for the field, a willingness to learn, and some aptitude for the work. Always be looking to learn new things, read new books, and try new things. Be open to listening and trying different approaches. Someone like that will quickly gain a huge amount of experience and become an invaluable member of the team. However, a person with lots of experience who is not willing to learn anything new is nearly useless in a rapidly changing field.

By the same token, there is much you can do to prepare for a career in video game design. You do need to gain some experience, whether it's on campus or during an internship. This is one field where having hands-on experience is a must. The most important first step is to get an education that prepares you for the job.

Loving to play video games is a good first step, but there's much more you need to do to prepare for a career in gaming.

2 PREPARING FOR A CAREER IN VIDEO GAME DESIGN

A re you interested in and excited by the idea of creating video games that users love to play? Are you open to learning new technologies, enjoy constant change, and want to be on the cusp of what's new and exciting? Do you have some degree of mathematical prowess, feel comfortable learning upper-level math, and enjoy learning how to program? What about creativity and imagination? If you feel that you have all or even most of these traits, then video game design is a good career for you. Remember that you can develop and improve your creative muscle on the job.

Since you've picked up this book, you probably already have an idea that a career in video game design is what you want to do. This chapter covers the educational background and skill set necessary to get started in the field. Before you begin, keep in mind one of this chapter's main takeaways: *Get practice and experience creating video games wherever and however you can.*

Experience, even if it's simply creating and designing your own mobile game apps for your friends to try, will help you realize your dreams more easily. A demo reel or design portfolio, which showcases your work, is an important element that employers look for in potential video game designers.

Career opportunities for video game developers are expected to grow more than 27 percent from 2010 to 2020, which is much faster than average job growth in the United States. Also, a recent news report showed continued growth of video game sales despite a weak national economy. The profession of video game developer always rates very high on the scale of job satisfaction as well. Video game design is a fun and satisfying career that's here to stay and only shows promise of growth in the future.

PURSUING THE RIGHT KIND OF EDUCATION

You read in Chapter 1 that you'll typically need a bachelor's, or four-year, degree either in computer science or some kind of multimedia graphics to have the best chances of securing an entry-level position as a video game designer. Although there isn't one specific degree that video game designers have to pursue, a college curriculum that best meets video game designer requirements usually blends computer and game design theory with modern programming languages.

In fact, many degree programs can lead to video game design employment, including computer programming, computer science, and art/design or visual communications with an emphasis in video game design, which is also called art applied multimedia. You can also take the more lucrative, and safer, computer-programming route by learning C and C++. If you're focusing more on the design/art side as a degree, computer certifications, such as in Java, C++, and Adobe Flash, are particularly helpful. Adobe Flash is a multimedia software program used to create graphics, animations, and games that are played and viewed in the Adobe Flash Player.

> ""
> *My response [to someone asking how to become a video game designer] would be to suggest they either study programming or art. Programming is a necessity in this industry, but a background in programming can lead to a lot of opportunities in areas of project management. All video game designs need several different kinds of art, so it doesn't really matter if an artist specializes in 3-D or 2-D media.*

ARSENY LEBEDEV, SIGNUS LABS

Although it's definitely more difficult, you may be able to snag a video game developer position without those credentials if you have technical skills and practical experience. In this case, you need to have an exceptional body of work to show to potential employers. However, to increase your chances of getting that first job, and for better advancement once you're there, it's best to have a degree. The bottom line is that having a four-year degree is going to make you more marketable when you're looking for your first job.

Remember that gaining hands-on experience creating games and using the applicable programming languages is your primary goal, no matter which educational path you pursue. Once you are in college, an internship in video game design or programming is worth pursuing, as it can help you build your demo reel and possibly lead to that first job. Use your university to make connections and find internships. Meet and work with other like-minded students in order to make those connections last.

CHOOSING A MAJOR: COMPUTER SCIENCE OR MULTIMEDIA ART AND DESIGN?

What major should you pursue? Although there is no standard path to becoming a game designer, most people employed in the industry agree that a computer science degree is a great, safe option. Likewise, it's important to have a broad education in fine art and humanities. For that reason, many people suggest a dual major with computer science and digital art, or perhaps a major/minor combination. Related fields such as architecture, engineering, and cinematography all can be used in designing a game. Each teaches you how to make good building designs for your game, teach realistic physics, and are related to cinematic cut scenes. Computer science, however, will provide you with the best base for game design.

Other majors that are directly applicable to a career as a game designer include game art, game design, game development, computer animation, multimedia art, and graphic art and design. Be careful about some of the "short-cut game design" majors. Many of them aren't worth much. General wisdom in the industry states that a computer science or multimedia design degree at an accredited school is much better than the current "game design" offerings out there. This may change as schools and universities

It's always best to choose a major based on your natural interests and skills.

see the need to build specific curricula for this expanding field, but in the meantime, do your research.

Of course, there are also examples of game designers who have graduated with bachelor's degrees in unrelated fields but know that their skills are exceptional. In fact, a frequent comment in the industry is that excellent skills and experience in the form of a great demo reel always trump formal education, or lack thereof.

The program and class options available to you will depend on the school you select. With that framework in mind, build a combination of major and minor courses that complement your strengths and interests. This will likely be a mix of computer science and digital art.

Be sure to pick a degree path relevant to your pursuits. If you are examining the pros and cons of different majors, think about the skills that you are lacking and find courses through which you can develop your talents, whether it's computer science, multimedia, 3-D graphics, or other classes.

Regardless of the path you choose, you do need to feel comfortable learning programming languages and high-level math concepts. That's true even if you choose the game artist or developer path. To learn more about what you need and what to study, check out Get In Media's website (getinmedia.com/careers/game-designer), which explores the skills and education necessary for a career as a game designer and where to begin.

CHOOSING A UNIVERSITY/EDUCATIONAL PATH

There are only about thirty colleges and trade schools that offer degrees specifically in game development, but this isn't your only option, or even perhaps your best one. Many more schools offer degrees in computer programming, computer science, and art and design with an emphasis in video games. These are all suitable stepping-stones into video game design. A degree in computer science, for example, will give you a much broader perspective and a strong base of job-related skills than one specifically tailored only to game design.

You can also take classes online. Search for "video game programming classes" to get started. However, before you sign up and give anyone your money, make sure you evaluate the program carefully. Make sure it's legitimate, too. Get help from a parent and guidance counselor. It's easy to get scammed if you're not savvy about your investments. Check out Game Institute's website, gameinstitute.com, as a start.

THE LAST WORD: ATTEND COLLEGE OR NOT?

If you're debating whether you should attend college or not, research and answer these questions:

- How would a degree improve your current skill set?
- Do you need the structure that school provides to keep motivated and on track?
- Would being in school hinder your pursuit of real-life experience, or would it open doors for it?
- How do you compare to the video game developers who have the jobs that you want?

There are other aspects of degrees that will set you apart. Although many of the things you learn with a college degree might not translate directly to your day-to-day job duties, you will be learning invaluable, important life lessons and strategies that make you a better person, and therefore a better employee. These include but aren't limited to becoming more organized, less selfish, more open-minded, more knowledgeable about the world in general, getting perspective on your views and outlook, building skills in rhetoric and persuasion, learning how to work with people who are different from you, and becoming more independent. These are "soft" traits that you will theoretically develop as you age and mature regardless, but immersion in college jump-starts and accelerates this growth. In addition, college can be an incubation place for creativity, and you just might meet your future business partner in your dorm.

Although a degree isn't for everyone, it can be a great path to get you where you want to go, especially when you pair it with real-life experience. Also, many large companies won't even look at your demo reel and résumé unless you have some kind of accredited degree.

BUILDING A MARKETABLE SKILL SET

Video game designers who have programming skills and multimedia modeling skills are best equipped to find good jobs right away. Optimally, you'll want to understand languages such as C++, Java, and Objective-C, as well as be familiar with a scripting

language such as Lua. As you learn and practice, you should be building a demo reel that showcases your knowledge of these languages and tools, as well as your creative application of them in the form of great games, levels, and so on. This section explores the basic technologies you need to learn and use as a designer.

LEARNING TO USE C++

As you have already read, C++ is the most widely used object-oriented language, especially in console video games. Many great tools have been developed for it. However, it is large, complicated, and can be difficult to learn. There are great tutorials on the Internet for getting started in C++ that include hands-on exercises and steps that you follow to build a simple program. Simply search online for

"C++ tutorial" or "learn C++ for gaming." Two great tutorial websites to get you started are learncpp.com and cplusplus.com.

A great beginner's book can take you a long way, too. You might consider starting with Michael Dawson's *Beginning C++ Through Game Programming*, third edition. Written for the beginning game developer or programmer, Dawson approaches learning C++ from the perspective of gaming. Check out your local library for this or related titles. Look for books that teach C++ specifically from a game-programming perspective.

Since C++ is complex and can be difficult at first, some people are better off starting in the more structured environment of the classroom. With that said, take as many C-specific courses as you can at your school or even at the university satellite or tech school in your area. The good news is that you have time on your side, so you can approach learning C++ as an ongoing project that you do in your spare time. Entering college with a working knowledge of C++ will place you ahead of the crowd!

LEARNING TO USE OBJECTIVE-C

Objective-C is the primary programming language used when writing software for the Mac OS and iOS platforms. It's a superset of the C programming language and provides object-oriented capabilities. Objective-C inherits the syntax, types, and statements of the C language and adds syntax for defining classes and methods. Once you're comfortable with basic object-oriented concepts and the C/C++ language, you can begin to learn Objective-C. At that point, it will be relatively easy to learn.

Again, the best first place to explore Objective-C is online. There are great hands-on, step-by-step tutorials online. Simply search for "Objective-C tutorial" or "learn Objective-C." Two great websites to get you started are cocoadevcentral.com/d/learn_objectivec and codeschool.com/courses/try-objective-c. Another excellent resource is Apple's own developer site: developer.apple.com. Search that site for updated Objective-C information. Keep in mind that you'll have better success if you learn C or C++ first, before you begin to conquer Objective-C.

LEARNING A SCRIPTING LANGUAGE

Scripting languages are programming languages that are used to control other applications. In games, they are specifically embedded into the game in order to run external "scripts," or pieces of code that can be modified without recompiling the entire game. This is useful because it makes programmers more efficient by reducing the amount of time they spend waiting for their code to compile. It also enables players to write their own scripts, resulting in much more complex and interesting modifications, or mods. Which of the numerous scripting languages out there should you try first?

Lua is the most commonly used scripting language in designing games from *Aquaria* to *World of Warcraft*. Because Lua is so popular, it has special libraries that make it easy to embed in C++ programs. Python and JavaScript V8 are two other simple scripting languages that are used often in the gaming world.

To get started with Lua, check out this Lua programming tutorial on YouTube: youtube.com/watch?v=li44LQoxOuU. It is one of the better and easier-to-understand tutorials online. Of course, things change at light speed on the Internet, so you can always search for "Lua tutorials" and find one that suits your fancy.

USING A GAME ENGINE

A game engine offers a flexible and reusable software platform that provides all the core functionality required to develop a game. The term arose in the mid-1990s, especially in connection with 3-D games such as first-person shooters. Id Software's *Doom* and *Quake* games were so popular that rather than work from scratch, other developers licensed the core portions of the

GameSalad allows even the novice to quickly create video games using a drag-and-drop interface.

software and designed their own graphics, characters, weapons, and levels—the "game content" or "game assets."

Unity, one of the more popular game engines, is a cross-platform game engine that uses C++ and has a built-in IDE. It is used to develop video games for web plug-ins, desktop platforms, consoles, and mobile devices. The free version of Unity includes publishing support for iOS, Android, Windows Store, Windows Phone, BlackBerry, desktop, and the web, as well as a thirty-day trial of Unity Pro.

BUILDING YOUR DEMO REEL/DESIGN PORTFOLIO

Having a demo reel/design portfolio is important when pursuing a career in game design. It's never too early to start building one. Reels should show evidence of scenes, levels, or complete games that you've designed or contributed to as a team member.

Rock Stars in the Industry

As part of educating yourself about the industry, it's smart to be aware of and follow leaders and trendsetters. The point of following people who are successful in the industry is that, along with learning about and seeing the hottest trends and approaches, you'll learn how successful people present themselves out in the video game design world. You can emulate their behaviors, learn from their games, and then forge your own path to success. Don't be afraid to go online and find games that speak to you personally, and follow their designers as well.

Shigeru Miyamoto: An iconic video game director, producer, artist, and designer, Shigeru Miyamoto is responsible for many of the most adored and popular games and characters in the industry, including *Mario*, *Donkey Kong*, *Zelda*, and *Yoshi*. He was the first person to be inducted into the Academy of Interactive Arts & Sciences' Hall of Fame in 1998, and in 2007, *Time* magazine selected him as one of the 100 most influential people of the year.

Sid Meier: Sid Meier designed the breakthrough strategy game called *Civilization* in 1991. The Meier brand is one of the most well-known names in the video game world. His current studio, Firaxis, is working on a console-friendly version of the *Civilization* series. Meier was the second person to be inducted into the Academy of Interactive Arts & Sciences' Hall of Fame.

Yu Suzuki: Yu Suzuki has been creating games for Sega since 1985, including *Space Harrier*, *Out Run*, *After Burner II*, the *Virtua* series, and, more recently, *Shenmue*. In the past, when Nintendo and Sega were big rivals, Suzuki was referred to as the counterpart to Shigeru Miyamoto. His *Virtua Fighter* series has been recognized by the Smithsonian Institute for its contribution to the field of Arts & Entertainment. Suzuki was inducted into the Academy of Interactive Arts & Sciences' Hall of Fame in 2003.

SimCity creator Will Wright.

Will Wright: The creator of the *SimCity* series, *The Sims* series (the best-selling PC game of all time), and *Spore*, Will Wright is also one of the founders of Maxis, which is now part of Electronic Arts. Widely regarded as one of the key figures in gaming, technology, and entertainment, he was inducted into the Academy of Interactive Arts & Sciences' Hall of Fame in 2002.

John Carmack: From the primitive graphics and gameplay of *Commander Keen* to the immersive, multiplayer, first-person shooter environments of *Quake* and *Doom*, John Carmack has always been at the cutting edge of video game programming and design. He was inducted into the Academy of Interactive Arts & Sciences' Hall of Fame in 2001 and placed number two in *Develop* magazine's survey of heroes. In 2010, he was further honored with the Lifetime Achievement Award at the Game Developers Conference.

These are just a few of the many video game pioneers. There are also many up-and-coming gamers out there, both men and women, who might not be in the legendary category just yet but are accomplishing amazing things. Be sure to do your "homework" and find ones that speak to your style and approach. As a start, bookmark and visit gamasutra.com, which keeps its finger on the pulse of the video game development industry.

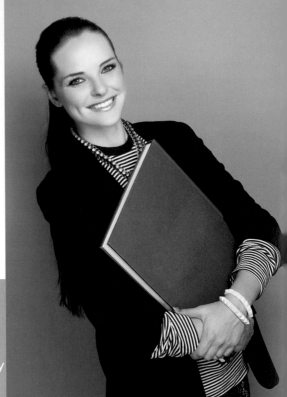

Building a portfolio of your work and experience is important, no matter how meager it seems at first. Be sure to update it frequently with your best work!

A portfolio is appropriate for those who want to enter the field as artists, animators, or 3-D modelers.

Even without a "real" full-time job, there are lots of creative ways to start to build something that showcases your work. Here are a few suggestions to get you started.

Start making games! This might seem obvious, but you won't start learning and honing your skills until you get out there and start making games. To begin, use software with a shorter learning curve such as Twine (twinery.org), Stencyl (stencyl.com), or GameMaker (yoyogames.com/studio). All have free versions and require no code.

For your very first game, you should shoot for what developers call a prototype: a smaller version of your idea with a few working mechanics. A prototype lets you see how your game plays, allows you to improve the design, and forms the foundation that you can later build on to make a full game. You can also add levels to

> # " "
> *Prototyping is an essential skill. Prototyping is to game design as storyboarding is to the visual artist or filmmaker.*
>
> —WILL WRIGHT, LEGENDARY VIDEO GAME DESIGNER OF *THE SIMS* SERIES

existing games as a way of honing and showing off skills. Always test your work and share it online.

The next step toward building your body of work is to get real-life video game designing experience by scoring an internship or apprenticeship with a video game design company. Many video game companies offer internships and apprenticeships for qualified students. You won't earn a lot of money as an intern or apprentice, but the experience you gain will be a huge step in your career. You also will have the opportunity to make contacts with people in the industry. Internships and apprenticeships aren't always widely advertised, so it's a good idea to actively search for them.

Regardless of the methods you use, you should be continuously updating your demo reel with new and improved game bits. As you gain experience, your demo reel will improve and become more interesting. Also, continually updating your reel shows that you're actively working to hone your skills.

Making Your First Video Game App

The first logical step you can take right now is to start creating gaming apps. After you make something that is fun for you and your friends to play, you can load it to one of the app stores and maybe even make some money.

Keep in mind that your first few games might not go viral or make you a millionaire, but these are your first steps toward learning the craft. All you need is the desire and a game plan. Follow these steps for best results:

1. **Study and learn the app marketplace.** To begin, check out the Apple App Store and Google Play, which are loaded with various categories of games. Study the successful apps and play them, and figure out what people want and what kind of apps they are downloading.

2. **Design your app.** This is when you create the design document, a type of outline that lies between a résumé and a battle plan for your game. A design document details everything about the design of your game including the gameplay, the mechanics, the character, the plot, and the scene. It also shows everything that needs to be done, who will do it, what the expectations are, and the general timetable for getting completion.

3. **Prototype your idea.** Your prototype should be a real but smaller version of your idea. Ask yourself questions such as, "How will players progress through the game?" and "How will players interact with the world?" Your prototype could include graphics or screenshots, as well as audio and music cues. The idea is to show how the app will look and where everything will be placed.

4. **Register as a developer.** Once you have sketched out your idea, the next step is to sign up as a developer. Register with the platform for which you're looking to create apps.

5. **Begin coding.** Choose a game engine for your game. Engines require tools, which are sometimes included but sometimes need to be created, that allow you to interact with and create the game within the engine. Then you'll need to find someone who knows how to script in that engine, or learn to do it yourself. This usually requires a certain amount of programming skills.

6. **Create content.** Start creating the actual game content. This includes modeling the characters, creating the environments, the objects that the player interacts with, making the game sprites, meaning a sprite that lives in a game, whose function it is either to help or destroy the user, and so on. Skills with 3-D software and visual arts are usually needed to complete these tasks. If your game is fairly complex, this is an area you might want to send to another developer or use third-party templates, at least until you gain more experience.

7. **Test the app.** Test, test, and test again. You need to go through every possible scenario in your game to make sure that there are no bugs. Ask several friends and family members to do the same. This takes time and manpower. Be sure to allow lots of time for testing.

8. **Enter the market.** There are many places where you can release your game, but the app stores and the site called Steam (store.steampowered.com) are the most open to newcomers. You could release your game independently on your own website, but hosting costs tend to be high. You'll also have less visibility.

This list might seem intimidating to you at this stage, but keep in mind that the simpler your concept is, the easier each of these steps becomes. Also, just because the concept of a game is quite simple doesn't mean it won't do well. The app Flappy Bird is a prime example of that! As you gain experience, your game ideas will probably grow in complexity.

This is the best way to get experience right now, at your age. Every game you make means experience, which is what you need and probably lack at this stage in planning your career. You never know, a game you create now could lead to an internship at your dream company.

Tips for creating your demo reel/portfolio:
- Include only your best work
- Start and end with your strongest pieces
- Tailor the demos to your dream job
- Know your strengths—focus on them
- Keep it short and simple
- Get feedback from others

Don't:
- Include work for which you don't have approval
- Include work that you don't love to do
- Worry about adding music
- Add elements to fill space
- Include work that's not yours

One final piece of advice: Specific video game designer requirements vary depending on the company or internship to which you are applying. Find out what they are well in advance of submitting your application. This way you can include the correct materials and put your best foot forward.

INCREASING YOUR ODDS OF SUCCESS

If you take only one thing away after reading this chapter, let it be this: The key to setting yourself apart is a successful blend of education and experience. As you pursue your degree, you also need to seek out practical experience. Your demo reel or design portfolio is an important element that employers look for in would-be video game designers.

Learn programming languages and build your demo reel every chance you get. This should sound like a fun prospect to you. If the thought of building your demo reel with levels and games you've created makes you groan, you probably shouldn't be in this industry. Your demo reel/portfolio will set you apart, regardless of your degree. The more on-the-job experience you acquire, the less your degree will matter to potential employers.

> ## " "
> ## *If you never stop learning,*
> ## *you will never stop seeing*
> ## *the possibilities.*
> ### —BILL GATES

Your experience will also give you a solid foundation as to the challenges and goals of video game design. It will allow you to "talk the talk" with potential employers. With a solid foundation of the current technologies, you can more easily adapt to the next cool program or approach that exists on the horizon for video game design.

The final "secret" to success is that you need to have a passion for the work. Having a passion for your job will make it so much more fun, and potential employers will pick up on your enthusiasm. Passion also leads to creativity.

Throughout your career, you also must keep up-to-date on new tools and computer languages. If you have a real passion for video game design, this will happen naturally, as long as you keep an open mind and actively pursue new venues. Education is a lifelong pursuit. It doesn't stop after you graduate. In fact, you'll likely learn far more about video game design on the job than you ever do in the classroom. Keeping this in mind, you might wonder what the day-to-day job really looks like. Read on to find out!

Being able to collaborate and work well with others are important skills for game developers.

3 A DAY IN THE LIFE OF A VIDEO GAME DEVELOPER

V ideo game development is a fast-moving, multi-billion dollar industry. Creating a game from concept to finished product can take as long as three years and involve teams of up to 200 professionals. There are many stages to the end product, including creating and designing gameplay, animating characters and objects, creating audio and video, and programming, testing, and producing the game.

This chapter explores the tasks performed by a typical video game designer. It breaks down the broad job titles and delves into specialty areas describing each in greater detail. All of the different variations of video game design have their benefits and drawbacks. It's smart to understand them—based on your personality, strengths, and goals you want to find your best fit.

Let's assume that you've followed all the advice from the previous chapters and have the education and experience you need. You have also put together a great demo reel. If you have completed these steps, you have positioned yourself in the market well. Your next step is to find the right environment to showcase your skills and work toward your goals.

BEFORE YOU PUT YOURSELF OUT THERE

Before you start looking for that perfect professional fit, it's important that you take some time to evaluate and understand your work goals, personality traits, and needs. Even though you might not find the exact job that fits all your characteristics right away, it's still a valuable process to go through. If nothing else, knowing what you want and who you are will come across in an interview and can very likely set you apart from many other candidates. An air of self-confidence shows the interviewer that you have thought about your career and the "big picture," so to speak.

The questions that follow are a good place to start. You might not be able to answer them all right now, as some of these questions will become clearer as you gain experience, take classes, and build your demo reel. The answers you give will also undoubtedly change with your personal and professional growth. It's therefore important to revisit these questions as you gain experience, knowledge, and perspective.

Keep in mind that there are no wrong answers, and it's vitally important that you answer honestly and realistically.

- What are your career goals? Do you want to become an expert in a certain industry? Do you want to work for the best-known video game development company out there? Is your goal to one day become the "boss"? Do you want to learn as much as you can about game programming or learn enough so you can some day start your own company? Are you looking to build a career that allows you flexible hours and complements your busy life? Think about what you want from your job and career, and be honest.

- Do you feel comfortable taking on a project with very little guidance and few guidelines, or are you more likely to succeed when you have solid guidelines and procedures for completing a project?

- How likely are you to share your ideas with others in a group when you think they're good ones? Do you think it's better to keep quiet at first and make sure you understand all the variables, or are you more likely to jump in with your ideas and make them known?

- Do you feel comfortable in risky situations, ones that might jeopardize your standing but might also have great payoffs? Or are you more successful and comfortable in less risky settings?

- Does direct competition with others bring out your best efforts, or are you more likely to shut down when you feel an environment is too competitive and not collaborative?

- Do you enjoy sweating the details, so to speak, or are you more motivated by the "big picture" of any project?

- If you had to pick only one path, would you rather become an expert in only one particular area or be somewhat well versed in many areas of your profession?

- Do you enjoy brainstorming new and different ways to solve problems or reach goals, or do you feel better going with the established methods?

This is just a sampling of the questions asked on career aptitude tests. The point of these questiona is to measure certain personality characteristics and match them to careers that complement those traits. If you are still struggling with finding the best career for you, check out the more complete tests you can take online. A great choice is the *Psychology Today* online Career Personality & Aptitude test. You can find it on psychologytoday.tests.psychtests.com.

THE BASIC JOB DESCRIPTION

Hopefully, you now have some idea of your career and
educational goals and you have a realistic understanding of your
strengths and weaknesses. This section sets the groundwork for
the basic job duties you'll have as a video game designer. The
tasks and responsibilities listed here are all inclusive. This means

you won't likely be responsible for all these aspects of the work, particularly if you are employed by a large company, where job titles are more strictly defined.

Game developers are involved in the creation and production of games that range from computer, handheld, console, and arcade games, to those on the Internet, mobile phones, and other wireless game applications.

Designers, producers, and graphic artists all contribute to the final game. Programmers and software developers turn the idea into code, which provides the game with its operating instructions. The work involves either design, including art and animation, or programming. Game and software developers create the core features of a video game. The general duties of a game developer, which is a general all-inclusive term that encompasses all of these job titles, include the following:

- Developing designs and/or initial concept designs for games, including charts and diagrams that outline the various concepts and components involved

- Creating story lines, game scripts, and character biographies

- Conducting design reviews

- Designing role-play mechanics

- Creating prototypes for staff and management

- Creating the visual aspects of the game at the concept stage

- Producing the audio features of the game, such as the character voices, music, and sound effects, including using 2-D or 3-D modeling and animation software

- Programming the game using programming languages such as C++, and documenting that specific code

- Preparing digital graphics, animations, sound, video, photographs, and images for editing

- Combining structural, mechanical, and artistic elements into the game's environment, such as buildings, vehicles, and decorative finishes

- Quality-testing games in a systematic and thorough way to enhance their capabilities, find problems or bugs, and recording precisely where the problems were discovered

- Documenting the entire game design process

Keep in mind that you won't be responsible for all of these functions, especially if you're just entering your first job. Entry-level and junior game programmers typically use basic tools and languages, such as C++, to add small elements to games. They are also expected to keep up with changing technologies. Lead developers and programmers write more complicated code and manage other programmers.

General skills that you need to develop in order to succeed in this industry include the ability to:

- Solve complex technical problems that occur in the game's production

- Effectively convey knowledge to colleagues, clients, publishers, and gamers

- Understand complex written information, ideas, and instructions

- Work closely and well with team members to meet the needs of a project

- Plan resources and manage both the team and the process

- Be creative and have artistic flair

- Have a commitment to understanding and using new technologies

- Understand color and form as it relates to multimedia

- Perform effectively under pressure and meet deadlines to ensure the game is completed on time

As you read the descriptions in this section, note which areas get you excited and those in which you have little or no interest. This is part of finding your passion. Although you might not be able to do it all at once, you need to know where your passion lies and acquire skills in those areas.

Of course, how much you do of any of these tasks depends greatly on your area of specialization. Many, if not most, of the entry-level positions aren't particularly specialized. Initially you'll be coding bits of code and contributing to level programming. However, you want to figure out which specialization(s) you prefer and begin developing your skills and abilities in that area.

VIDEO GAME DESIGN JOB SPECIALIZATIONS

The title of video game developer covers a broad area of work. For one, game developers usually specialize in a particular game platform, such as PlayStation, Xbox, or Nintendo, for example, and a particular aspect of game development, such as programming artificial intelligence or designing gameplay.

Beyond the game platform you choose, there are many job specializations within the game development industry, including but not limited to:

Quality Assurance Tester: A quality assurance tester is responsible for monitoring and testing technical standards in gameplay, including the graphics, sound, and functionality during game development. They assist programmers in finding bugs, or errors, and work with the team on performance-related issues. These are often the easiest entry-level positions to score.

Programmer: The programmer position itself has various specialties, such as network, engine, tool chain, scripting, and artificial intelligence programming. Programmers write code, usually in C++ programming language, or use game-development engines to create the video games. In essence, they create the code to make the game work.

> # "Low-level programming is good for the programmer's soul."

Audio Engineer/Digital Video-Sound Editor: The audio engineer, or digital video-sound editor, is involved in the computer-based editing of the game's video sound. Working under instruction from directors, these editors make decisions in regard to the mood, pace, and climax of sound effects. This involves working closely with other professional staff to analyze, evaluate, and select sound effects for integration with images and other media.

Artist: The artist position is usually broken into several specialties, including concept artist, animator, and 3-D modeler. The artists create the game's visual characters, objects, and scenery, and produce concept art and drawings, called storyboards, at the planning stage. A technical/3-D artist creates and manipulates images and models using 2-D and 3-D computer graphics software, usually in Adobe Photoshop, Maya, or 3DS Max. They work closely with animators and concept and layout artists to design and model characters, vehicles, buildings, and other objects present in the gaming environment.

Producer/Director: The producer/director manages, plans, oversees, and in some cases funds the development of a game.

Starting off as a quality assurance tester or game programmer is a good way to get your foot in the door.

They work closely with the marketing department and the team developing the game, ensuring schedules, budget, and productivity targets are met. The industry's more seasoned individuals usually hold this position.

Designer: The designer decides what a game looks like and how it plays. Depending on the company and the position level, they either come up with their own original ideas or work from an existing concept.

Special Effects Technician: The special effects technician creates special effects, animation, or other visual images using film, video, computers, or other electronic tools and media for use in the game.

Animator: The animators bring the characters, objects, and scenery to life with computer modeling and animation software during the production stage. This includes arranging characters

The Sega Corporation headquarters in Tokyo, Japan.

and objects designed by the technical artists in a sequence of different positions to give the illusion of movement. Animators work with programmers to create interactive sequences and work with testers to provide lifelike movements through digital techniques, such as motion capture.

In all of these roles, except the one of producer/director, you would report to a producer or project manager tasked with overseeing the entire process. Producers/directors also ensure

that the finished game is completed on time. Again, it's smart to begin thinking now which area or areas interest you the most, and which ones best complement your skills. With that in mind, you can build your demo reel based on those specializations.

The scope of the entry-level video game designer position can vary greatly depending on where you work. The next section can help you find the kind of company culture that best fits your personality, goals, and skills.

CHOOSING THE RIGHT KIND OF COMPANY

As you read earlier, you're more likely to be successful and happy if you find a setting that matches your goals, needs, and personality traits. Keep in mind that these company descriptions are generally true, and for every rule, there is an exception. As always, do your homework and find out about the companies to which you are applying. Do they have the kind of company culture that complements your personality?

An important caveat is that one of the most consistent complaints from video game developers are the insanely long hours they are expected to work, day in and day out. That might be something you need to resign yourself to when you start out, regardless of the company that employs you.

This is the entertainment industry, so game designers have to have a creative mind and also have to be able to stand up against the marketing people at their company, otherwise they cannot be creative. There are not that many people who fit that description.

SHIGERU MIYAMOTO, ICONIC VIDEO
GAME DEVELOPER

"And that is what happens when we resist change."

The video game design field will morph many times over during your career, and you need to be open and ready to change along with it.

WORKING FOR A LARGE COMPANY

As mentioned briefly, larger companies tend to have solid defined job titles for each department and division. These jobs also are more likely to be highly specific and segmented to a particular task or skill. That means you'll come in at an entry-level position with a very defined job description. You'll also likely be closely managed and mentored by someone called the lead developer, who explains to you the overall concept of the game to which you will contribute. In a large corporate setting, you're much less likely to be in the position to pitch your own creative ideas or develop your own characters and scenes for consideration.

The benefits of a job like this are that you have very established guidelines and a clear path to success. There is less uncertainty in what your employer expects from you, or what you need to do to complete a project. You're more likely to have established guidelines and procedures for getting work done, and you're more likely to get consistent and detailed training in using the software and programs you'll be needing (which are often the best and most recent versions out there).

In addition, you'll more likely be able to take courses and certifications, and further your education at the company's expense. The perks overall, such as health club memberships, better health insurance, more liberal vacation policies, and more, are also better at larger companies. Generally speaking, job security is higher with larger companies. Also, it never hurts to have the experience of working for a well-known organization on your résumé, especially when you're starting out.

Perhaps the more important benefit is that you're surrounded by a great number of like-minded individuals who are more experienced in the industry. You will learn a lot in this type of environment, which has been fine-tuned, in theory, by the years of experience and knowledge brought to the table by your coworkers.

The drawbacks are probably evident by now. There is potentially a certain amount of monotony in these jobs, and you're not always rewarded for thinking in new and creative ways. The "status quo" more often rules the day. Your job will be very specific to one or a few certain programming tasks, so you need to be able to thrive in that environment. If you are uncomfortable taking risks and feel more at ease when given clear instructions for accomplishing a task, a larger corporation may be a good fit for you.

WORKING FOR A SMALLER COMPANY

Working for a smaller company can be a great experience, one that can expose you to all aspects of video game design. It can also be frustrating, political, and stressful. Smaller firms also tend to be more supportive, less bureaucratic, and more willing to hire workers embarking on new careers.

In a smaller setting, you are more likely to be able to get your hands dirty in many different aspects of video game design, depending on your interests. You'll be exposed to a diverse range of activities and even get more involved in the day-to-day running of a business.

Smaller teams and a less regimented setting mean that employees get to try their hand at various skills. They are more likely to be open to new ideas, more likely to take risks, and more likely to be collaborative. Your creative ideas have a much better chance at being considered. There is a strong possibility that you may be working alongside senior employees, which provides great opportunities for learning from these seasoned professionals. This is particularly great for someone just starting out.

If you find yourself in the market and really want that big-picture experience of being involved in every aspect related to video game design, it is better to be at a smaller company. However, one of the biggest problems with many smaller organizations is that there is a lot of office politics and nepotism, and this can create hostile and difficult work environments. Larger corporations tend to have strict policies about how people are hired and promoted, but they can still have their own brand of office politics.

The other drawbacks of working at a smaller company include fewer perks and less job stability. These companies don't have the money to throw around that bigger organizations do, which means you might not be able to further your education or get certifications with the company's financial support until you've been there a while, or maybe not at all. Also, you might be using older software and devices.

If you are more comfortable taking risks, prefer to have a breadth of knowledge rather than a depth of one design topic, want to contribute your ideas right away, or are more motivated by the "big picture" of any project, a smaller company or nonprofit is a better fit.

Do your homework and research the office culture before you accept a position at a small firm. Find out if people are generally happy there, and why or why not. This is something you should do regardless of the company's size, but the impact of the culture at a smaller organization will be greater on your own job satisfaction.

THE BEST COMPANIES IN THE INDUSTRY

You can ask ten different people and read ten different video game design articles and you'll receive ten different answers about which are the best companies to consider for employment. The good news is that there are several great video game companies out there, and many more are on the rise. Those listed here were chosen based in part on longevity, reputation, and overall employee satisfaction. When you visit their websites, you can see which genres of games they create, learn a bit about the culture, and of course, view their online job postings.

- **Riot Games.** Established in 2006 and based in Santa Monica, California, the Riot Games company rates highly on many different lists as a great place to work. Its only game title at this time is *League of Legends*. See riotgames.com.

- **Valve Corporation.** Founded in 1996 by two former Microsoft employees and currently based in Bellevue, Washington, Valve Corporation also ranks highly on employee satisfaction lists. Titles include the *Half-Life* series, the *Left 4 Dead* series, *Team Fortress*, and *Counter-Strike*. See valvesoftware.com.

- **Zynga.** Founded in July 2007 and headquartered in San Francisco, California, Zynga creates social media games such as *FarmVille*, *CastleVille*, *CafeWorld*, and *Mafia Wars*. Zynga's workplace reputation has soared high and dipped low since making its presence in the marketplace. The company's offering of great benefits and exciting working conditions are positives, but very long work hours are a common complaint among employees. See zynga.com.

- **BioWare.** BioWare is a Canadian video game developer (founded in February 1995) currently owned by the American company Electronic Arts. Titles include *Dragon Age*, *Mass Effect*, *Neverwinter Nights*, and *Star Wars: The Old Republic*. Their offices are located in Edmonton and Montreal, Canada, as well as in Austin, Texas. Employee reviews of working conditions are mostly positive. See bioware.com/en.

- **Activision.** Founded in 1979 with U.S.-based offices in Santa Monica and Foster City, California, the long-standing Activision company makes games for almost every platform. Their long list of titles includes *Cut the Rope*, *Angry Birds*, the *Call of Duty* series, *SkyLanders*, and the *Guitar Hero* and *Band Hero* series. Employee reviews are generally positive. See activision.com.

- **Blizzard Entertainment.** Founded in 1991 and based in Irvine, California, Blizzard Entertainment is currently a subsidiary of the company Activision Blizzard. Titles include the *World of WarCraft* series, the *StarCraft* series, and the *Diablo* series. Employee reviews are generally positive. See us.blizzard.com/en-us.

Of course there are many more video game design companies than those listed here. Do more research on your own. One important site to explore is glassdoor.com. This is a website-based "career community" where people can read reviews about companies, all posted by people who worked there. This site will provide you with more insider information about the culture of companies. Posted on the site are company reviews, CEO approval ratings, salary reports, interview reviews and questions, office photos, and more. One of the most consistent complaints about video game companies is the very long hours employees are expected to work. Keep in mind that comments at glassdoor.com are added anonymously. It's possible that some former employees who may be disgruntled wrote a few of the postings, yet it's still a good site for viewing candid comments from current and former employees.

INCREASING YOUR ODDS OF SUCCESS

Regardless of where you end up working, there are certain skills and traits you should develop to increase your odds of performing well. To be successful in the working world of video game design, you need to:

- Be adaptable and able to pick up new techniques and technologies

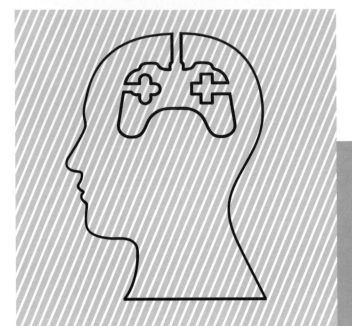

Having a head for gaming is great, but make sure you are honing your communication and inter-personal skills as well.

- Have good interpersonal and communication skills
- Be able to work on your own or with a team
- Be able to tap into your initiative and creativity, even when under a tight deadline

Recognize the areas where you naturally struggle, and make efforts to improve in them. In particular, being open to learning new things and taking new approaches is critical in this field. If this isn't something that comes naturally to you, practice it. You can and should develop these skills over time. You want to have the best overall combination of skills and experience so that no company will turn you down. You also want to be able to earn the highest pay offered for your position.

Video Game Design

Ninety percent of what is considered 'impossible' is in fact possible. The other ten percent will become possible with the passage of time and technology.

HIDEO KOJIMA, VIDEO GAME DEVELOPER OF THE *METAL GEAR* SERIES

Be sure to consider cost of living when you determine the salary you need to live.

4 BENEFITS AND SALARY

B y now you should have a pretty good idea about the educational path you need to follow to become a video game developer, including how important it is to get experience creating games as soon as you can. You should also have a picture in your mind about what video game developers do on the job and how that job differs in various organizations and markets. Ultimately, you should have a feel for whether it's something that sounds interesting and exciting to you. If you've made it this far, you probably do think it's something you would like to do for a living. In this chapter, how that living is made and the typical salary and benefits earned by video game designers across the United States are discussed.

Keep in mind that, just like cost of living, salaries, and to a lesser degree benefits, vary greatly across the United States. From coast to coast and big cities to smaller towns, it's vastly different. If you want to live and work on either coast, particularly in the high-profile cities such as New York, Los Angeles, or San Francisco, your cost of living will average 30 to 40 percent more, your salary should generally reflect that. Conversely, you may not be offered as high a salary to work in a large Midwestern city or smaller town, but the cost of living there will be significantly less, Chicago excluded, which means your salary will be worth more, relatively.

Before you begin your job search, look closely at the areas in which you would like to live. For example, how much does it cost to rent an apartment in the desirable, fun area where people your age like to live? You'll need to have a realistic understanding of how far the salary offered will go. However, before we get into the nitty-gritty details about money, let's discuss the other "intangibles," or the benefits and perks your company will offer to you as part of full-time employment.

WHAT YOU CAN EXPECT IN TERMS OF CORPORATE BENEFITS AND PERKS

The types, sizes, and amount of benefits vary greatly across the board, but the good news is that companies in the tech field offer some of the most liberal and generous benefits available, and they typically cater to younger people. This means that these benefits are more likely to be things you'll enjoy receiving. As a reminder, you almost always have to be a full-time employee to enjoy a company's benefits. If you accept a part-time job or take on contract work, the company benefits aren't usually part of the package. Make sure you understand what is and isn't included when you accept a part-time or contract position.

Also, keep this general truism in mind that the larger the company, the better the benefits package. This is generally true because larger companies, as well as public sector government employers, have more money in their coffers, but there are exceptions to every rule. Many newer tech companies take an innovative approach to offering benefits as a way to attract talent, and you could very well find a smaller start-up with a great benefits package.

BENEFITS YOU WILL MOST CERTAINLY RECEIVE

Benefits you will most certainly receive as a full-time employee in the United States include health insurance of some kind and a predetermined number of sick and vacation days. The amount, cost, and extent of these benefits can vary greatly.

According to the U.S. Bureau of Labor Statistics, the average number of annual paid holidays is ten. The average amount of vacation days is 9.4 after a year of service. If this is somewhere you see yourself staying for a while, consider not only the number of vacation days in the first year, but also how that number increases as you accumulate years in the company.

Almost half the (medium and large) employers surveyed by the U.S. Bureau of Labor Statistics offered either a defined benefit or a defined contribution pension plan, such as a 401K, where you save some of your earnings into a retirement account. Many employers will match the amount you put into retirement up to a certain percent. About 75 percent of companies offer health insurance, but almost as many require employees to contribute toward the cost.

Note that smaller companies are much less likely to have contribution pension plans and to offer health insurance. As the kinks are ironed out of the Affordable Health Care Act, not having health insurance from your company may be less of a concern. You should, however, be insured in one form or another. As a young person, you might not think that health insurance is important for you, but one car accident or injury could mean tens of thousands of dollars in medical expenses if you're not covered.

BENEFITS AND PERKS YOU MAY BE OFFERED

Benefits and perks that are common in the high-tech fields and that you might have access to include paid educational programs and/or certifications, flextime and casual work environments, and special offerings such as gym memberships. Of these, the most valuable in terms of pure dollar benefit is the chance to further

Many employers offer gym memberships as one of the perks of employment.

your education at the company's expense. Whether it's pursuing your master's degree or getting certified in C++ or some other game design technology, your educational efforts will make you more marketable and valuable at your current job, as well as down the line. Tuition reimbursement can largely benefit you in two ways. You save money by not having to pay for the classes, which is a big savings, and you stand to earn more in the future because greater knowledge increases your value.

Of course, there may be "strings" attached, usually in the form of some employment agreement to stay at the company a certain amount of time after your education is complete. This is more likely to be the case when you're pursuing a long-term degree such as a master's, rather than taking a series of classes to become certified in an area. Also keep in mind the word "reimbursement." You will likely need to pay for the classes initially, and only after you have completed the class and received a grade or rating deemed acceptable by your employer will you be reimbursed. Even with the qualifications, it may well be worth it. As always, do your homework so you know what you're getting into.

Especially in the fast-paced and ever-changing world of video game development, it is critical that you keep up-to-date with trends and technologies. Having your company on board with this, monetarily and philosophically, is incredibly valuable.

> *The video game market is huge, and the ability to tell stories, and tell different kinds of stories in the gaming space, is quickly evolving and changing for the better.*

JIM LEE, COMIC BOOK
ARTIST AND WRITER

In terms of the other perks and benefits, keep in mind that nearly all tech companies offer casual dress these days. They might tout it as something unique and special, but it is increasingly becoming the norm. Being able to set your own work schedule, called flextime, or have the option to telecommute some days also falls under the "casual work environment" umbrella. It's up to you to decide how valuable these perks are and look for the ones that really matter. For example, if you work out on a regular basis, look for employers who offer gym memberships. Having paid access to a local gym is more of a norm these days, especially on the coasts.

It's important for you to consider which perks would complement your lifestyle and your needs and choose accordingly. If you don't plan on having children for a while, it's not that important whether on-site childcare is offered.

Above and Beyond: The Special Touches

Innovative companies have become increasingly creative in providing perks and benefits that will attract the types of employees they want. If you find a company boasting a culture that embraces your passions and interests, it's a win-win.

Benefits don't just stop at day care, flex-hours, and tuition reimbursement. Consider this long list of real perks that actual companies offer in today's market:

- Convenient services to make the other parts of your life hassle-free, such as on-site dry cleaning, concierge services, take-home meals, on-site meals delivered to your desk, and use of company vehicles.

- Bring your pet to work, every day!

- Fitness-related points programs where employees are rewarded for activities such as participating in running and walking campaigns. Employees then redeem the points for fitness items, such as running shoes, golf clubs, and jogging strollers.

- Paid leave for special traveling or service projects. For example, Patagonia, the outdoor-apparel maker, gives employees two weeks of full-paid leave to work for the green nonprofit of their choice.

- In-house educational programs and other perks are open to relatives of employees.

- Brainstorming allowances, whereby employees are permitted to spend up to 10 percent of their time on research projects of their own devising.

As an example specific to the gaming market, Zynga provides employees with free lunches and dinner all week, as well as free snacks. They also boast relaxation lounges with Nintendo, arcade games, Xbox 360, and PS3 gaming systems. If you really want to relax, you can schedule an appointment for massage, reflexology, and acupuncture therapies, all on site.

You can expect a fast-paced, collaborative environment when you work in game design!

Parents, on the other hand, should check to see if the company provides paid time off when a child is sick. If you're not a morning person, ask about flexible hours. If you can't stand wearing a suit, ask about the dress code.

It's important to ask about perks, too, because not all will be offered to all employees, nor will they be mentioned during an interview. The perks that a company offers tells you something about what they value, another insight into the company culture. As you read earlier, it is important to find a company that meshes with your goals, interests, and needs.

SO, HOW MUCH WILL YOU MAKE?

It's tricky to say exactly what you should expect to make when you first enter the market, because salaries for video game designers vary widely, especially among independent contractors. As you read earlier, your salary will depend greatly on where in the country you work and the subsequent cost of living there. It's in your best interest to do your homework and research the cost of living in the area you're considering and to become familiar with the competitive starting salaries there, all before you're made an offer.

The International Game Developers Association (IGDA) lists four types of game designers, including basic game designers, lead designers, level designers, and fiction or screenwriters. Each position is tasked with a different role in the ultimate design of a video game and each draws a salary accordingly.

IGDA reports that entry-level video game designers make between $50,000 and $80,000 annually, with the average being $57,500. The highest reported salary was $200,000.

LearnDirect career advice lists the starting salary for video game artists and programmers at about $37,000 a year. Experienced designers and lead programmers and producers earn around $85,000. These salaries don't include bonuses that many companies typically offer for time-sensitive project work.

Animationarena.com, a site that tracks animation-related news and provides links to animation-related education, also lists salary ranges for various game design positions. 3-D animators, for example, make between $50,000 and $60,000 annually, whereas game programmers with 3-D skills make up to $55,000. The entry-level annual pay for a lead programmer is close to $56,000. Once you have at least three years under your belt, you'll be averaging about $83,000 a year. After you have been in the business for more than six years, your annual salary will be over $90,000. Project managers and producers with experience make between $80,000 and $100,000. An executive producer makes up to $130,000.

The video game field is a lucrative one, but you'll likely have to start at entry-level wages like everyone else.

On the other side of the coin is the video game tester, which can sometimes be an excellent entry-level position or a good way to get experience during the summers while you're in school. It isn't, however, as good a career path choice. Video game testers don't get the exposure to the bigger picture that can help advance their careers. Their salaries start around $18,000 and top out around $55,000 annually for experienced lead testers. These jobs are often temporary, which means no health insurance or benefits.

Industry pressure and trends can cause wages to ebb and flow. When a new console is introduced, for example, it often increases pressure on wages as companies rush to expand the number of game titles available for that system.

So, you might be wondering if you can negotiate your salary. If this is truly your first job, the short answer is no. With little experience and being "low on the totem pole," so to speak, you're not likely to be in the position to negotiate a better salary. If you have some extraordinary experience, or something that is particularly desired by this specific company, you may be the exception. However, most companies, particularly large and mid-sized, have standard packages that they offer to newbies and they don't stray very far from those offerings. If you feel that you have something extraordinary to offer, you may have more luck negotiating better benefits or perks, such as a greater number of vacation days or access to the tuition-reimbursement program much sooner than it's normally offered.

THE END OF THE LINE!

You should now have a much better idea about what video game developers do and how you can become one. If you're still interested in a career in video game development, congratulations! The goal of this book was to provide you a clear path to making your career dreams happen. To increase your odds of success along the way, keep these points in mind:

- **Start making games now.** You can start by creating a mobile game app and testing it out on friends and family. Be sure to check out and use the free tools on the Internet. Practice and learn as much as you can.

- **Educate yourself.** Whether it's about the market, the technologies, the schools, or the companies, do the research and be "in the know." You'll make better decisions and give better interviews.

- **Be positive but realistic.** The video game development market is competitive and working for others can be trying at times. If you have a passion for the work, you can and will succeed.

- **Build your interpersonal communication skills.** No matter what you end up doing for a living, you'll do it better when you can deal with people calmly and positively.

- **Find a company whose culture matches your interests.** When you believe in what you're doing, it makes everything easier.

Above all else, discover your passion and live it. This is sometimes easier said than done, but if you accomplish it, your work will never seem like drudgery, and you'll be a happier person to boot. Good luck in your career searches!

People measure success differently. Find your passion and do that for a living. Your work will seem more fun that way!

GLOSSARY

application programming interface (API) Specifies how computer components interact with each other. In object-oriented languages such as C++, the API includes a description of a set of classes, with a set of behaviors associated with those classes. The API is like a group of all the kinds of objects you can create from the class definitions and their possible behaviors.

casual games Games with limited complexity tailored for shortened or spontaneous playing. Includes social media-type games and found largely in the mobile market.

cloud computing Model of software sharing where users access the software from a "cloud" (a network of remote servers), rather than have a copy of the software on their local devices. Cloud providers install, operate, manage, and update the software for their clients. Also called *Software as a Service (SaaS)*.

codebase The whole collection of source code used to build a particular application or game. Typically, codebase includes only human-written source code files, not source code files generated by tools.

debugger A computer program used to test and debug another program in order to identify any programming-language-specific errors, or "bugs," which the programmer can then fix.

design document A template-like document that outlines all aspects of the game's design, gameplay, interface, and world. Usually includes text, images, diagrams, concept art, or any media that illustrates the design decisions. Some design documents include prototypes of a chosen game engine. Game designers update the design document continuously throughout development.

GLOSSARY

first-person shooter (FPS) A type of video game that involves gun and projectile weapon-based fighting from a first-person perspective. The player typically experiences the action through the eyes of the good guy, or the protagonist, and in some cases, the bad guy, or the antagonist.

integrated development environment (IDE) A programming module that's packaged as an application program, usually with a code editor, a compiler, a debugger, and an interface builder. IDEs provide a user-friendly framework for many modern programming languages.

Kickstarter Crowd-funding site whereby you describe your idea through the site's project pages and seek funding from independent backers. Gaming was Kickstarter's biggest funded category in 2012, raising $83 million for successfully funded projects.

massively multiplayer online game (MMO or MMOG) An online video game that can support many players at the same time, where players cooperate and compete with each other, and sometimes interact with people in the game's world. By necessity, they are played on the Internet. MMOs are created on most network-capable platforms, including PCs, video game consoles, and smartphones and other mobile devices. Examples include *Happy Farm*, *Anarchy Online*, and *World War II Online*.

memory management The process an application or programming language goes through of controlling and distributing memory, by assigning pieces called "blocks" to running resources to optimize overall performance. Memory management ensures that memory is available for the various objects and data structures at all times.

object-oriented programming (OOP) language
A programming language model organized around objects rather than actions and data rather than logic.

random access memory (RAM) The most common type of memory found in computers and other devices and is synonymous with main memory. It's the memory available to programs.

read-only memory (ROM) Special memory used to store programs that start up a computer or device and perform diagnostics. Most PCs have a very small amount of ROM.

reverse-engineering Breaking a program down in order to understand it, create a copy of it, or improve it. Reverse-engineering is especially important with computer software, as programmers can take machine language code (zeroes and ones) and reverse-engineer it back into the C++, for example, that it was written in, and then copy the program.

source code The statements and code in a language such as C++ or Java before it is compiled into machine code, which is the code that is read by the computer. A programmer writes a program in a language such as C++ (that's the source code). Before a computer can do anything with that program, it must be translated, or compiled, into a machine-readable language, which is comprised only of numbers, for the computer to read.

version control The process of managing changes to documents and/or programs. Changes are typically marked by a number or letter code, which is called the revision number. Version control is an important aspect of collaborative projects, including game development.

SOURCE NOTES

INTRODUCTION

(1) pg. 5: The Gaming Evolution, "National History Education Clearinghouse," teachinghistory.org/history-content/ask-a-historian/25764.

(2) pg. 5: The Gaming Evolution, "National History Education Clearinghouse."

(3) pg. 6: The Gaming Evolution, "National History Education Clearinghouse."

(4) pg. 7: Webdesigner Depot, "Video Game Design Between 1990 and 2008," www.webdesignerdepot.com/2008/12/video-game-design-between-1990-2008.

(5) pg. 8: Webdesigner Depot, "Video Game Design Between 1990 and 2008."

(6) pg. 8: "30 Years in the Making: The Evolution of Video Game Design," www.youtube.com/watch?v=EACNI6N0ICU.

CHAPTER 1

(1) pg. 11: "*CNNMoney*, Best Jobs in America," money.cnn.com/pf/best-jobs/2013/snapshots/15.html.

(2) pg. 14: Liedholm, Marcus, "The Famicom Rules the World! – (1983–89)," web.archive.org/web/20100101161115/http://nintendoland.com/history/hist3.htm.

(3) pg. 15: Weesner, Jason, "On Game Design: A History of Video Games," www.gamecareerguide.com/features/327/on_game_design_a_history_of_video_.php?page=3.

(4) pg. 15: "Atari Files For Chapter 11 To Separate From French Parent," www.prnewswire.com/news-releases/atari-files-for-chapter-11-to-separate-from-french-parent-187698581.html.

(5) pg. 15: Molina, Brett, "Atari Resets with Jump Into Social Casino Gaming," www.usatoday.com/story/tech/gaming/2014/03/26/atari-social-casino/6915065/.

(6) pg. 17: Tairne, EJR, "The Making and Unmaking of a Game-Maker Maker," gamasutra.com/blogs/EJRTairne/20130504/176610/The_Making_and_Unmaking_of_a_GameMaker_Maker.php?print=1.

(7) pg. 18: Stark, Chelsea, "How to Successfully Fund Your Game with Kickstarter," mashable.com/2014/01/25/kickstarter-video-game.

(8) pg. 20: "Video Game Design Career Paths," Creative Uncut, www.creativeuncut.com/video-game-design-career-paths.html.

(9) pg. 24 PULL QUOTE: Video Game Design Schools, "An Interview with Arseny Lebedev," www.videogamedesignschools.org/an-interview-with-arseny-lebedev.

(10) pg. 24: Games from Within, "So You Want to Be a Game Programmer?" gamesfromwithin.com/so-you-want-to-be-a-game-programmer.

(11) pg. 26 PULL QUOTE: Design3, "Advice for Aspiring Game Developers," www.design3.com/industry-insight/promotional-videos/item/2406-advice-for-aspiring-game-developers.

SOURCE NOTES

CHAPTER 2

(1) pg. 30: *CNNMoney*, "Best Jobs in America: Video Game Designer," money.cnn.com/pf/best-jobs/2013/snapshots/15.html.

(2) pg. 30: Fox News, "Video Game Sales Soar Despite Weak Economy," www.foxnews.com/story/2008/08/15/video-game-sales-soar-despite-weak-economy.

(3) pg. 30: "So You Want to be a Game Programmer?" Games from Within. gamesfromwithin.com/so-you-want-to-be-a-game-programmer.

(4) pg. 31 PULL QUOTE: Video Game Design Schools, "An Interview with Arseny Lebedev," www.videogamedesignschools. org/an-interview-with-arseny-lebedev.

(5) pg. 33: "Game Designer," Get In Media, getinmedia.com/ careers/game-designer.

(6) pg. 34: "How to Program Video Games," www.gameinstitute. com.

(7) pg. 38: Wolfire Games Blog, "Choosing a Scripting Language," blog.wolfire.com/2010/01/Choosing-a-scripting-language.

(8) pg. 39: "Free Unity Download," Unity Website, https:// unity3d.com/download.

(10) pg. 43 PULL QUOTE: "design3 - Advice for Aspiring Game Developers," www.youtube.com/watch?v=sLULgSDSogI.

(11) pg. 43: How Stuff Works, "Required Skills for a Video Game Designer," electronics.howstuffworks.com/video-game-designer1. htm.

(12) pg. 44: "Demo Reels: What It Takes to Get Noticed," Digital-Tutors, www.digitaltutors.com/11/demoreel.php.

(13) pg. 40: "Top 10 Tuesday: Game Designers," www.ign.com/articles/2007/07/24/top-10-tuesday-game-designers?page=2.

(14) pg. 40: "Top 10 Tuesday: Game Designers."

(15) pg. 41: Ku, Andrew, "The Top 15 Best-Selling PC Games Of All Time," www.tomshardware.com/picturestory/587-best-selling-game-list.html.

(16) pg. 41: "Top 10 Tuesday: Game Designers," www.ign.com/articles/2007/07/24/top-10-tuesday-game-designers?page=2.

(17) pg. 41: "Top 10 Tuesday: Game Designers."

(18) pg. 41: "Top 10 Tuesday: Game Designers."

(19) pg. 45 PULL QUOTE: "Never Stop Learning," evancarmichael.com/Famous-Entrepreneurs/556/Lesson-5-Never-Stop-Learning.html.

CHAPTER 3

(1) pg. 51: "Career Personality and Aptitude Test," *Psychology Today,* psychologytoday.tests.psychtests.com/take_test.php?idRegTest=3242.

(2) pg. 54: "Game Developer: Job Description, Duties and Requirements," education-portal.com/articles/Game_Developer_Job_Description_Duties_and_Requirements.html.

(3) pg. 56 PULL QUOTE: "John Carmack Quotes," Brainy Quote, brainyquote.com/quotes/authors/j/john_carmack.html.

(4) pg. 54: "Game Developer; Job Description," prospects.ac.uk/ games_developer_job_description.htm.

(5) pg. 59: "Jobs Guide: Games Developer," The Job Guide Site, jobguide.thegoodguides.com.au/occupation/Games-Developer.

(6) pg. 60: "Shigeru Miyamoto Quotes," brainyquote.com/quotes/ authors/s/shigeru_miyamoto.html.

(7) pg. 44: "How to Make a Video Game," WikiHow.com, wikihow. com/Make-a-Video-Game-from-Scratch.

(8) pg. 64: "Riot Games," riotgames.com.

(9) pg. 64: "Valve Corporation," valvesoftware.com.

(10) pg. 64: "Zynga," zynga.com.

(11) pg. 64: "BioWare," bioware.com/en.

(12) pg. 65: "Activision," activision.com.

(13) pg. 65: "Blizzard Entertainment," us.blizzard.com/en-us/.

(14) pg. 67 PULL QUOTE: "Hideo Kojima Quotes," polyvore.com/ gdc09_hideo_kojima_inspirational_quotes/thing?id=11667797.

CHAPTER 4

(1) pg. 70: "Compare Cost of Living," FindTheBest.com, cost-of-living.findthebest.com.

(2) pg. 71: U.S. Bureau of Labor Statistics, "Vacations, Holidays, and Personal Leave: Access, Quantity, Costs, and Trends," bls.gov/ opub/perspectives/issue2.pdf.

(3) pg. 71: U.S. Bureau of Labor Statistics, "Vacations, Holidays, and Personal Leave: Access, Quantity, Costs, and Trends," bls.gov/ opub/perspectives/issue2.pdf.

(4) pg. 73 PULL QUOTE: "Jim Lee Quotes," brainyquote.com/ quotes/authors/j/jim_lee.html.

(5) pg. 75: "12 Tech Companies That Offer Their Employees the Coolest Perks," thenextweb.com/insider/2012/04/09/12-startups-that-offer-their-employees-the-coolest-perks.

(6) pg. 77: "How Becoming a Video Game Designer Works," electronics.howstuffworks.com/video-game-designer3.htm.

(7) pg. 77: "Video Game Salary," Animationarena.com/video-game-salary.html.

(8) pg. 78: "Video Game Tester Salary," gameindustrycareerguide.com/video-game-tester-salary.

BOOKS

Berntzen, Katherine. *In Pursuit of My Success for Teens: Developing a College, Career, and Money Plan for Life*, 2nd ed. Naperville, IL: Katherine Berntzen, 2011.

Dawson, Michael. *Beginning C++ Through Game Programming*, 3rd ed. Boston, MA: Cengage Learning, 2011.

Kennedy, Sam R. *How to Become a Video Game Artist: The Insider's Guide to Landing a Job in the Gaming World.* New York, NY: Watson-Guptill, 2013.

Peterson's Publishing. *Teens' Guide to College & Career Planning*, 10th ed. Lawrenceville, NJ: Peterson's Publishing, 2011.

Rogers, Scott. *Level Up!: The Guide to Great Video Game Design.* Hoboken, NJ: John Wiley & Sons, 2014.

WEBSITES

GameDev.Net
www.gamedev.net

Explore this online community for game developers of all levels, from the beginner to the seasoned industry veteran. More than 850,000 developers worldwide take advantage of the developer news, thousands of articles and other resources, and active forums offered.

Game Industry Career Guide

www.gameindustrycareerguide.com

This site offers advice on kick-starting your career in video game development. Take advantage of the guidance offered in résumé-building, applying to companies, networking, interviewing, and finding the best schools. Check out the latest salary information on various game developer positions.

Mapping Your Future

www.mappingyourfuture.org

Explore more career options and map out your goals. Learn tips on résumé writing, job hunting, and job interviewing.

Monster

www.monster.com

Perhaps the most well known and certainly one of the largest employment websites in the United States. Fill in a couple of search boxes and away you go. You can sort by job title as well as by company name, location, salary range, experience range, and much more. The site also includes information about career fairs, advice on résumé writing, interviewing, and more.

Occupational Outlook Handbook

www.bls.gov/oco

Produced by the U.S. Bureau of Labor Statistics, this website offers lots of relevant, updated information about various careers including average salaries, how to work in the industry, the job's outlook in the job market, typical work environments, and what workers do on the job.

BIBLIOGRAPHY

Berntzen, Katherine. *In Pursuit of My Success for Teens: Developing a College, Career, and Money Plan for Life*. 2nd ed. Naperville, IL: Katherine Berntzen, 2011.

"Career Personality and Aptitude Test." *Psychology Today*. Accessed March 26, 2014. psychologytoday.tests.psychtests.com/take_test.php?idRegTest=3242.

"Game Developer: Job Description, Duties and Requirements." Education Portal. Accessed May 1, 2014. education-portal.com/articles/Game_Developer_Job_Description_Duties_and_Requirements.html.

Games from Within. "So You Want to be a Game Programmer?" Accessed April 24, 2014. gamesfromwithin.com/so-you-want-to-be-a-game-programmer.

"How Becoming a Video Game Designer Works." HowStuffWorks.com. Accessed May 5, 2014. electronics.howstuffworks.com/video-game-designer3.htm.

"How to Create a Gaming App." WikiHow.com. www.wikihow.com/Create-a-Gaming-App.

"How to Make a Video Game From Scratch." WikiHow.com. www.wikihow.com/Make-a-Video-Game-from-Scratch.

Jozefowicz, Chris. *Cool Careers: Video Game Developer*. Pleasantville, NY: Gareth Stevens Publishing, 2010.

Kennedy, Sam R. *How to Become a Video Game Artist: The Insider's Guide to Landing a Job in the Gaming World*. New York, NY: Watson-Guptill, 2013.

"Occupational Outlook Handbook: Web Developers." U.S. Bureau of Labor Statistics, 2012 data. Accessed March 17, 2014. www.bls.gov/ooh/computer-and-information-technology/web-developers.htm.

Sessler, Adam. "30 Years in the Making: The Evolution of Video Game Design––Adam Sessler Interviews Mark Cerny." Accessed April 16, 2014. www.youtube.com/watch?v=EACNI6N0ICU.

"Vacations, Holidays, and Personal Leave: Access, Quantity, Costs, and Trends." U.S. Bureau of Labor Statistics. Accessed April 2, 2014. www.bls.gov/opub/perspectives/issue2.pdf.

Weesner, Jason. "On Game Design: A History of Video Games." Game Career Guide. Accessed April 20, 2014. www.gamecareerguide.com/features/327/on_game_design_a_history_of_video_.php?page=3.

INDEX

Page numbers in **boldface** are illustrations.

ABOUT THE AUTHOR

KEZIA ENDSLEY is an editor and author from Indianapolis, Indiana. She has been involved in the technical publishing field since the days of CompuServe, before the "real" Internet took off. She has enjoyed being a part of educating people of all ages about technical subjects for over two decades. In addition to editing technical publications and writing books for teens, she enjoys running and triathlons, reading, and spending time with her family.